Great Americana

Georgia Speculation Unveiled

Abraham Bishop

Georgia Speculation
Unveiled

by Abraham Bishop

READEX MICROPRINT

Foreword

In 1795 the Georgia State Legislature approved the "Yazoo Act," which allowed four companies to purchase approximately 35 million acres of western land in what are now the states of Alabama and Mississippi. The companies obtained the land for around one and a half cents an acre. Thus began the largest land speculation operation in United States history. However, popular indignation in Georgia caused the next legislature to void the grants in 1796 with a Rescinding Act. It is about these events that Abraham Bishop wrote in his *Georgia Speculation Unveiled*, 1797.

Speculators sought large tracts of unoccupied land which they could purchase cheaply and resell at great profit. The Yazoo land of the state of Georgia, virtually unsettled in the 1790's except for Indians, appeared ideal for this purpose, even though much of it was unsuited for farming. Every member of the Georgia Legislature but one acquired a personal interest in the speculation schemes. Consequently the Yazoo Act passed easily in 1795.

The fraudulent manner in which the speculators attempted to unload their often worthless lands onto innocent settlers caused a storm of protest. Grand juries in all but two counties of Georgia declared the Yazoo Act illegal. One member of the legislature barely escaped hanging by the irate citizenry. The United States Congress adopted a resolution condemning the action of the Georgia Legislature. Georgia's newly elected senator, James Jackson, an outspoken critic of the act, was persuaded to resign his senate seat and to become a member of the new Georgia Legislature. From that position he led a successful fight to get the Yazoo Act voided in 1796.

Bitter controversy continued, however. Influential northerners who had purchased stock in the land companies urged the federal government to have the Rescinding Act nullified. The issue was not settled until 1810, when the United States Supreme Court handed down a landmark decision upholding the original Yazoo Act and declaring the Rescinding Act of 1796 unconstitutional—the first time the Supreme Court had declared a state statute to be unconstitutional. In 1814 the United States Congress indemnified the holders of grants to the Yazoo land, since Georgia had surrendered that land to the federal government in 1802.

Abraham Bishop, a resident of New Haven, Connecticut, was clerk of the probate court there at the time he wrote this pamphlet. He was an ardent supporter of Jefferson and a frequent writer on political questions of the day. He was incensed that "men who never added an iota to the wealth or morals of the world...[were] plotting the ruin of born and unborn millions—aiming with feathers to cut throats, and on parchments to seal destruction." These persons, he said, "are the robbers of modern days." His slender book against the speculators is difficult reading because of the tangle of legal problems involved. However, the very complexity of Bishop's arguments suggests the helplessness of the unsuspecting settler when confronted by the legal chicanery of the speculators.

Thomas P. Abernethy provides a closer look at the Yazoo land companies in his *The South in the New Nation, 1789-1819* (Louisiana State University Press, 1961), pp. 136-168. A biography of Abraham Bishop is contained in the *Dictionary of American Biography*.

Georgia Speculation Unveiled

GEORGIA

SPECULATION

UNVEILED;

IN TWO NUMBERS.

By ABRAHAM BISHOP.

HARTFORD:

PRINTED BY ELISHA BABCOCK.

[*COPY-RIGHT SECURED.*]

1797.

THIS Pamphlet is an actual, though not a literal an-swer to the " STATE OF FACTS," *publifhed by the Georgia Companies. It contains the outlines of the prefent ftate of the Georgia bufinefs, and a brief fketch of the arguments on both fides, with fuch Commentaries as the compafs of the work would allow. The general tenor of it, efpecially that part which treats of the Chancery powers of our Courts, will be found applicable to the cafes of all, who have fuffered by any kind of Land fpeculation.*

STATE of FACTS,

———

"UNDER the term of GEORGIA WESTERN
TERRITORY is included all that part of the
" State of Georgia, which lies weſt of the head waters
" of thoſe rivers, which fall into the Atlantic ocean.
" Theſe lands are principally inhabited by three na-
" tions of Indians, the Chaċtaws, the Chickaſaws, and
" the Creeks,—of which nations the following is a
" ſummary charaċter.

" THE Chaċtaws, or flat-heads, are a powerful, har-
" dy, ſubtle and intrepid race of Indians, who inhabit
" a very fine and extenſive traċt of hilly country, with
" large and fertile plains intervening between the Al-
" abama and Miſſiſippi rivers. They have about 40
" towns and villages, and 4000 fighting men.—They
" have large plantations or country farms, where they
" employ much of their time in agricultural improve-
" ments, after the manner of white people.

" THE Chickaſaws are a nation of Indians, who in-
" habit the country on the eaſt ſide of the Miſſiſippi,
" on the head branches of the Tombeckbe, Mobille
" and Yazoo rivers. Their country is an extenſive
" plain, tolerably well watered from ſprings, and of a
" pretty good ſoil. They have 7 towns, and their
" number of fighting men is eſtimated at 575.

" THE Creeks inhabit the middle part of Georgia.
" They eminently deſerve the encomium of all nations
" for their wiſdom and virtue in expelling the uſe of

" *fpiritous liquors.* The firſt and moſt cogent article
" in all their treaties with the white people, is, that
" there ſhall not be any kind of ſpiritous liquors ſold
" or brought into their towns.—Inſtances have fre-
" quently occurred, on the diſcovery of attempts to
" run kegs of ſpirits into the country, of the Indians
" ſtriking with their tomahawks thoſe who attempted
" it, and giving the liquor to the ſand, not taſting of
" it themſelves. It is difficult to account for their ex-
" cellent policy in civil government : it cannot derive
" its efficacy from coercive laws ; for they have no
" ſuch artificial ſyſtem. They have 55 towns, beſide
" many villages, and their fighting men are about
" 5800.—They are a well-made, expert, hardy, ſaga-
" cious, politic people ; extremely jealous of their
" rights, and *averſe to parting with their lands.* They
" have abundance of tame cattle and ſwine, turkies,
" ducks and other poultry. They cultivate tobacco,
" rice, Indian corn, potatoes, beans, peas, cabbage, me-
" lons, and have a plenty of peaches, plumbs, grapes,
" ſtrawberries and other fruits. They are faithful
" friends, but inveterate enemies ; hoſpitable to ſtran-
" gers, and honeſt and fair in their dealings. *No na-*
" *tion has a more contemptible opinion of the white men's*
" *faith in general, than theſe people : yet they place great*
" *confidence in the United States, and wiſh to agree with*
" *them upon a permanent boundary, over which the ſou-*
" *thern States ſhall not treſpaſs.* The country which
" they claim, is bounded northward by about the 34th
" degree of latitude, and extends from the Tombeckbe
" or Mobille river to the Atlantic ocean (though they
" have ceded a part of this tract on the ſea coaſt, by
" different treaties, to the ſtate of Georgia.)
   " Of this weſtern territory, thus inhabited, the ſtate
" of Georgia by act of their legiſlature, paſſed January
" 7th, 1795, ſold about twenty-two millions of acres,
" to four different companies—viz.

" One tract to James Gunn, Matthew McAllister
" and George Walker, and their associates, called,
" *The Georgia Company.*

" One tract to Nicholas Long, Thomas Glascock,
" Ambrose Gordon and Thomas Cummings, and their
" associates, called, *The Georgia Mississippi Company.*

" One tract to John B. Scott, John C. Nightingale
" and Wade Hampton, called, *The Upper Mississippi*
" *Company.*

" One tract to Zechariah Coxe, Mathias Maher,
" and their associates, called, *The Tenessee Company.*

" Half a million of dollars was the purchase mo-
" ney :—this, or the greatest part of it, was secured
" by mortgages, which have been since cancelled.—
" But the state of Georgia now reclaims these tracts
" of land, alledging that the act authorizing the sale,
" is contrary to the 4th article of the constitution of
" the United States ; repugnant to the 16th and 17th
" sections of the 1st article of the constitution of Geor-
" gia ; and was moreover obtained by means of fraud,
" atrocious speculation, corruption and collusion.—
" Hence, by an act passed February 13th, 1796, the
" aforesaid act of January 7th, 1795, was declared
" null and void, and the grants, rights and claims de-
" duced from it, annulled and rendered void and of
" no effect."

Thus far my statement is probably correct, being
mostly taken from Doctor Morse's American Gazet-
teer.

Between the time of passing the granting act in
January, 1795, and of passing the rescinding act in
February, 1796, a great portion of these lands were
alienated by the Companies, and became the property
of purchasers in the middle and eastern states. These
sales were effected under the influence of a certain
pamphlet, entitled, " *State of facts, shewing the right*
" *of certain companies to the lands, lately purchased by*

" *them from the state of Georgia,*" and under the influence of certain other means, which will be noticed in the course of these numbers.

To save the inconvenience of frequent references and quotations in the following pages, it may be well to inform the reader, that relying on the statement of facts, published by the Georgia companies, I verily believed (till after the rescinding act) that the *fee* of the lands sold to the companies and by them to us, had been extinguished by the state of Georgia ; but that the Indians had a right of hunting and fishing, which would in time be abdicated or easily purchased ; as such a kind of right had formerly existed in this colony, and had been virtually recognized in the several treaties with different tribes. But after the rescinding act, it appeared that the right of the state of Georgia to the *fee*, was just such a right as the state of North Carolina had set up to Indian lands ; but which had been negatived unanimously by a committee of Congress, consisting of a member from each of the states. It also appeared that this setting up of a *fee* was pointedly opposed to the uniform policy of the United States, to the uniform declarations of Congress, and to the treaty with the Creek nation, concluded August 7th, 1790.

As the *fee* which was the substance of all these sales had failed entirely and did not exist, and as much money had been paid, and many notes been given, it became important to enquire whether the right of preemption was worth any thing.—On enquiry it appeared that the state of Georgia had a very *questionable right* to purchase lands (of three Indian tribes, who had no disposition to sell them) whenever Congress, (who denied the existence of this right) should grant them liberty to hold a treaty. The Massachusetts and Connecticut rights of preemption were undisputed, and they contemplated lands, which the policy of the U-

nited States would juftify them in purchafing, and
which the right owners were difpofed to fell ; but the
numbers, characters and fituation of thefe three nations, combined with the policy of the United States,
prefented a very powerful contraft in thefe Georgia
lands. Impreffed with thefe ideas, it occurred to me,
that if the Creek nation had fold to Long, Glafscock
and others, their right of preemption to the ftate of
Georgia, or the ftate of Connecticut, I fhould as readi-
ly have been an affignee of the claim, as with a know-
ledge of facts, have been a purchafer under the Georgia companies.

BUT the refcinding act led up fome ideas about
fraud, atrocious fpeculation, corruption and collufion,
practifed on the legiflature, which led me to confider
whether fome fuch practices had not been adopted at
the northward as well as the fouthward ; and on enquiry, it appeared that fome of the agents of the Georgia companies had conducted honorably—and have
not any intention of profits in this unfortunate and de-
lufive bufinefs :—but that others had eminently fuftained the characters of fraud and deceit in felling,
which they had acquired in purchafing.

FROM thefe premifes it appeared to me that men
who take money or notes for that which proves to be
nothing, efpecially under the above circumftances,
ought to refund.—And this fentiment, if true, will o-
perate in favor of all, thro' whofe hands thefe lands
have paffed, back to the members of the firft companies ; and the refcinding act has recognized this fentiment, by providing that the firft companies may re-
ceive back the money paid, and no one can oppofe the
operation of it, but thofe who are watching to make
fortunes out of the nothingnefs of this Georgia bufinefs ; and this number I hope (for the honor of hu-
manity) is very fmall.

REPEATED difclofure of thefe opinions has led me

to hear much logic and law-learning upon this fubjedt —much cenfure upon the ftate of Georgia—many re= marks upon what the legiflature might, could, or ought to have done.—But though my attention has been of- ten fufpended by the eloquence of great and learned men, on the fubjedt ; yet no one has convinced me that the *right of the ftate of Georgia to buy land* of the Creeks, Chickafaws and Chadtaws was ever worth a farthing.—No one has convinced me that the ftate e- ver had fuch right.—No one has proved that the fee of lands, and a right to buy the fee, are the fame thing. Amidft the variety of opinions and the indefinite ftate of this bufinefs, I have ventured to throw out the fol- lowing difcuffion, as the refult of my own convidtion ; and have fubfcribed it for the exprefs purpofe of a- voiding that confufion, which often refults from ano- nymous publications.

Georgia Speculation Unveiled.

No. I.

LET *the buyer look out,* is a maxim fuppofed applicable to all contracts where land is named ;—
but to the northern fales of Georgia land it can have
no application ; for thefe are not fales of *land,* as facts
now fhew ; and by the fellers were not intended to be
fales of *land,* but a mere floating imaginary right to
buy land—which partakes no more of reality than a
right to buy goods or horfes. The right to buy Indian land is at beft no more than a chattel, and is a
perfect non-defcript, unknown to all the writers upon
real eftate. It originated in avarice and power, and
never, *in this inftance,* has gained any other exiftence
than on paper.

THE State of Georgia claimed a right in fee to certain lands,—which lands were in fact fubject to an abfolute fee-fimple, in the right owners,—and faid ftate
acknowledged this fee, fubject to a particular kind of
ufufruct—which ufufruct was the abfolute undifputed
dominion and poffeffion of thefe owners, with an ancient, inherent and interminable right of doing with
it as they pleafed, without any hindrance or molefta-
tion from this claimant :—and this fee, dominion and
poffeffion of the right owners, guaranteed by the Uni-
nited States, and fecured by fevere laws from all fraud
and force on the part of the preemptors :—and to
crown all, this fame preemption claimed over the heads
of this fame ftate of Georgia by the United States, who
have an uncontrolable right to decide by judicial offi-

B

cers of their own creation on the right of preemption :
—and again, this ufurped preemption of the ftate of
Georgia, fecured from invafion by their own conftitution and pofitive laws, and guarded againft fraud and
deceit by all thofe general maxims which obtain and
are recognized in all fovereign ftates.

THE mind of man can proceed but one ftep further,
and yet retain one idea of lands or claims ; and this
ftep is prefented in the kind of right, which the Georgia companies claim to thefe lands. By the force of
fraud and corruption (as I fhall fhew hereafter) they
have broken through all the barriers, which fo perfect-
ly fecured the fee and poffeffion of the right owners—
and after obtaining the femblance of a granting act,
came forward, and by a printed pamphlet, entitled,
" *State of Facts*," &c. declared to all the world, that
they were the true and lawful affignees of the *fee* of
thofe lands, and to all the ufes of it, except a particular kind of ufufruct, called a right of hunting and fifhing of the Indians. Not one of the attributes of their
claim was of neceffity a matter of record ; and the
land could not from its fituation promife to any purchafer under them an office of record, where he might
refort for evidence of title ;—therefore every thing in-
ducing a fale muft be from the feller, and in all fuch
cafes, *let the feller look out, that he deceive not the buyer.*
'Tis a maxim of common fenfe and reafon, that whatever inducements the feller improves to draw money
from the buyer he fhall make true, or fuffer the inconvenience of their proving falfe ; for if he has tak-
en money for his own falfhoods, he ought to refund
it, whenever equity and good confcience demand it.—
And if this rule is not in the books, it ought to be placed there, by the fide of *caveat emptor*. Both parties
are to look out ; all men are to look out ; *but courts
are efpecially to look out, and fee that men get no gain by
cheating their neighbours ;*—and if in every cafe they

cannot find a precedent for doing right, let them, as Lord Hardwicke did, make a precedent.

THE frauds practifed in the negociation and fales of thefe Georgia lands, have been as numerous and complicated as the heart of man could conceive ; and the property now refting for decifion of the courts in confequence of them, is to an immenfe amount. The refcinding act of the ftate of Georgia has brought all thefe matters to a crifis, and one decifion of the fupreme court of the United States, may probably influence the decifions of lower courts. I fhall therefore proceed to difcufs,—1ft. the validity of this refcinding act—2d. the impoffibility of affecting it by any court or power in the United States—and 3d. the confequence upon all the notes depending on the fales under the granting act.

1. THE validity of the refcinding act depends on the power which paffed it.—This is the fovereign independent ftate of Georgia, having a right to make or repeal their own laws at pleafure, and this right wholly uncontrolable. When individuals deal with each other, there are courts to compel compliance with their contracts :—how far the policy of the United States will fuftain a citizen in a difpute againft a ftate, for monies due on ftate notes, or otherwife acknowledged, and whether a marfhall may fafely commit to prifon the governor, treafurer or fecretary of the ftate for a ftate debt, is befide my prefent object. This was a grant faid to be ftanding on records, whereof the legiflature had the control. Thefe records do not now exift ;—they are burnt, and the reafons are affigned on new records for deftroying the fame. I afk, what remedy have the Georgia companies? They cannot bring a writ of ejectment ; for none but the Indians are in poffeffion.—They cannot fue for the lands, but in the ftate where the lands lie ;—and whatever court tries the caufe, muft try it by the exifting laws of the ftate

of Georgia ; and no law exifts in favor of the companies.—Copies of record will not anfwer : if they would,
a fecretary might certify what on trial would ejeet all
the people of a ftate from every foot of their land.
The exifting laws muft be fuch as are recognized by
the people, legally reprefented ; and the legal reprefentatives muft have a right to declare their fenfe of
the laws.

IN various cafes a legiflature may declare a pretended act void—as whenever 'tis contrary to conftitution
—as where a lefs number was prefent at paffing it,
than is required to form a houfe—or where the fpeak-
er or prefident of the council was bribed to declare
that a vote, which was not a vote ; or where the voters
in favor of an act were interefted in the paffing of it ;
or where it was paffed by members not having taken
the neceffary oaths ; and in all cafes, where fraud and
deceit are combined between thofe who compofe the
legiflature, and thofe who are to be benefited by any
particular act. Take this power from a legiflature,
and where is the fovereignty of the ftate ?—Such a
powerlefs ftate would be left open to the ravages of all
the unprincipled men in the univerfe, and their property and rights might be bartered for bribes. All
contracts with fovereign ftates muft be made in confidence that power and integrity will be united ; and
he who approaches a fovereign people for grants, muft
do it with clean hands. The maxims of honor and
honefty, which form a part of the policy of all enlightened fovereignties, are a fufficient guarantee to thofe
who deal uprightly with governments. Let thofe who
maintain a different doctrine, go profecute the national affembly { f France to make good their affignats, or
the United States for their continental bills.—Where
is the power to try the caufe ?—Or let fuch point out
the power, which can control the ftate of Georgia in
the enaction of their laws, or the management of their

records. Can the congrefs of the United States do it? Certainly no :—this would deftroy the confederation. Can the court of the United States? Clearly they cannot judge what laws ought to exift.

ALL the arguments of the oppofers to the refcinding act would be more plaufible, if they had in view real eftate in fee and poffeffion ; and had honeftly paid a fair confideration for it.—In fuch a cafe the law might ftretch its force to obtain them juftice ; but this being an unfubftantial thing the law cannot reach it, and could not do it, even if the queftion was between two individuals. As in cafe A owns a large farm, divided into 16 lots, and has a right to keep it and ufe it as long as he lives, and then to leave it to his heirs forever, B, C, D, and fo on, to the number of 16 ; knowing that competition of buyers raifes the value of farms, and difpofed for their own advantage to deprive A of this benefit, agree among them that B fhall alone bid on lot No. 1, C on No. 2, fo that A may fell to no other.—B fells his right of preemption in lot No. 1 to S for 10 dollars—S fells it to T for 100—T to U for 1000. Now B declares that he was cheated out of it, —that he never delivered the deed, &c. and that he holds himfelf a bidder for the land as much as ever. A is ftill in poffeffion, and likely fo to continue. Can U fuftain an action againft B? All men will agree that B has done U no damage, and U has gained nothing by his money ; but U has given his notes to T, and they are put in fuit.—He petitions for relief, ftating that T pretended that he owned the fee, and that it was the moft valuable part of the farm ; and that this was his inducement to give 1000 dollars ; that there were no records to refort to, and that he relied folely on T's word. T owns it all—and that in fact *he did not own the land, but had a right to buy it.* Will a court doubt what equity and good confcience demand in this cafe ?—To apply this, the land in queftion is merely a

right to buy land, which perhaps may never be for
sale ; which consideration alone, separate from the
doctrine of state sovereignty, is an invincible intrench-
ment for the state of Georgia, and the northern purchasers.

SOME say they may restore the records. Am I to
lie out of my money for an age, waiting to see whether the sovereign state of Georgia will pity me for
having been cheated by those who cheated her ? But
say others, she may grant it to another company, and
then we may try the title. Perhaps ages may pass before this sovereign state will grant it again, and then
neither of us can try the title to the lands, 'till the Indian title is extinguished.—That can't be done, but by
liberty to hold a treaty ; and this liberty cannot be
granted to those whom the state of Georgia denies as
her grantees, without violating her sovereignty ; unless by a suit at law the title should be determined ;—
and this title can never be made a law question, 'till
the fee and possession of the right owners is extinguished. Suppose a suit brought for the preemption,
what marshall could levy the execution ?—on what
could he levy it ? Whatever might be the judgment,
it would be an idle one, founded on nothing, and no
one could carry it into effect.

OTHERS say we have fairly bought it, *and will have
it*—and under this grant, rescinded and burnt, negoci-
ations are now making on the Missisippi lands. Vain
new editions of Missisippi dreams ! Such managers
might as well have used force without a grant ; but
when force is used, the reign of law and argument
has ceased.

THOSE who have not cheated nor been cheated in
this business, feel dispassionate ; they utter no depre-
cations against Jackson and his party, but calmly view
the state of Georgia, exercising a sovereign right in a
sovereign and righteous manner. A great class of

people comfort themfelves with a hope of trying the. queftion in the federal court, in fome one of the nor- thern ftates, whether the refcinding act is valid. As well might you try it before a juftice's court : the judg- ment of both would be equally powerlefs. Can you put at iffue in a diftant ftate the fovereignty of Geor- gia ? Can you obtain judgment that her legiflature has been diftracted; and what will you do with your execution ? All the propofitions which have been made to render the refcinding act of no validity are equally unpromifing, as to the prefent claimants under the gran- ting act.——All common-law principles attempted to be applied to the fubject are loft ; and the greateft lawyer is as the weakeft peafant, when attempting to difcufs it. As preemptive claims were never founded on law or right, they are not a fubject of law-books ; as they are peculiar to this country, they are not underftood elfe- where ; and as no cafes fuch as that of the refcinding act have ever before occurred, we are not to wonder, that men fhould be confounded at the operation of it.

BUT take the nature of their claims, as it is explain- ed—the rule of equity, which applies to the transfer of them—the fovereignty of the ftate—the refcinding of the act—the impracticability of trying the legality or equity of it, and it will fairly appear that *the prefent purchafers have nothing, and have no profpect of any thing for their money or their notes.*

2d. THESE things being true, what is the confe- quence upon the notes, depending on the fales under the granting act ? My anfwer is, that they ought not to be paid. What forms the courts may think proper to adopt in rendering them void is not material. If it be once afcertained that they ought to be void, courts will adopt or invent means proper for the end.

I BEGIN then by taking the three following pofi- tions—1ft. *That where a man has been deceived in a contract, and in confequence has deceived another, he fhall gain nothing by the transfer : If he escape without loss, it is the most he can desire.*—2d. *If he knew of the deceit practised on him previous to his selling, and yet made use of the deceit to induce a bargain, the least he can expect is the total loss of the price agreed on.*—3d. *If he were a partaker in the original deceit, he ought to lose the whole and be severely punished.* All the sellers of Georgia land have been within these classes ; for there was deceit at the bottom ;—and the many insidious arts practised by many of the sellers, give good reason to believe that they were the *original* deceivers.

THE whole transaction has all the air and appearance of a deep-laid and thoroughly executed plan of swindling.—The management of it proves that in the plan some southern people were to be gainers, and a great number of the northern people to be losers. I venture to predict, that some southern people will be bankrupts, and that the northern people will, after much vexation and delay, escape from loss. The rescinding act has struck a deadly blow at these first deceivers, and has arrested their career at the very moment when they were about to be loaded with wealth.

IN this precise stage of the business, the granting act being rescinded—the preemption resumed—no fee of lands in exiftence—the sellers greedy for payment, crouding for it at the bar of our courts—hosts of lawyers in their pay, on great wages—notes all in suit, and petitions for relief pending :—What can our courts do ? I answer, they are courts of law and equity, and are instituted for the purpose of doing right between man and man ; and this they are to do as far as may be, according to the principles and practice of law and equity in the books. I think it has been shewn abundantly, that this case could not have been contemplated in the books ;—it will follow then that this must form the basis of a precedent, and must be determined on its own merits.

THE firſt natural enquiry of the courts therefore, is—the character of the parties and their reſpective claims on the juſtice or equity of the law.—Not their private character ; but that which they wear in rela-ʼtion to this new and unprecedented cauſe.   The plain-tiffs in theſe cauſes when aſked this queſtion may ſafe-ly anſwer—" We are of thoſe, who contrived and col-luded with ſeveral members of the legiſlature of the ſtate of Georgia, to procure an act, violating their con-ſtitution and alienating the property of the people.— By promiſes of gain, by bribes, we led them to violate their oaths and thoſe principles of honor and fidelity to their conſtituents, which all laws command them to maintain.—We ſucceeded in our plan—procured a grant—we publiſhed not ſingle pages, but pamphlets of lies—circulated them with our own hands—ſup-ported them by our own affirmations—ſwore to them on our honor.—We thus enliſted men of integrity on our ſide—cauſed them to betray their neighbours— opened ſubſcriptions for the land—headed with names of men, whoſe permiſſion had never been obtained.— We entrapped the unwary—committed heads of fam-ilies for more than they were worth—pretended that we were ſelling under the influence of embarraſſment, for leſs than half what we might get, had we time to ſeek purchaſers.—We haſtened our bargains, left the reſcinding act ſhould overtake us ;—and to crown all, after we knew the act was paſſed, we employed emiſ-ſaries from Philadelphia to ride expreſs to complete bargains already projected, and to open contracts at all hazards ;—and when all this was known, we curſ-ed Jackſon and his party, in the language of fallen Lucifer to Michael.—We then ſecretly employed law-yers to write treatiſes againſt the reſcinding act, as their *voluntaries*, upon ſuch an unprincipled meaſure. —We circulated theſe to convince the dupes of our management, that Jackſon was an enemy to fair deal-

C

ing, and that the sovereign state of Georgia was a miserable subjected province, whose laws wanted no other confutation than our contempt:—but when conviction begun to operate on the public mind, and even on our own, that this rescinding act was serious and conclusive,—we employed hosts of lawyers, with enormous fees, to abet our cause;—and by their combined influence, and the aid of law-books, we hope to bear all before us. Tho' we knew that the men whom we had deceived, retained only the miserable shadows of land, which we pretended to sell them, and were willing to give up their deeds, and to suffer loss for their delusion—we haughtily refused; and to shew our power, loaded them with attachments—put them to all manner of expense, and are determined that wide-spread ruin and desolation shall follow those who have dealt with us,—for which object we approach the altar of justice, and pray the aid of this honorable court to carry our purposes into effect.—And if the court doubt this our character, we refer them to the rescinding act, containing 64 depositions in proof of it—to our pamphlets, and to our uniform conduct." To which character, well may the court say—Hail Lucifer, son of the morning!

THE other characters are plainly those, who have been the subjects of all this deceit, imposture, falshood and vexation; and who come before the court to obtain relief against a system of fraud and swindling—perhaps more complicated in its machinery, and varied in its operations, than any which has disgraced the character of man in this or any other age.

I HAVE put language into the mouths of the plaintiffs, which they would not be apt to use—*for 'tis the language of truth,*—not fancied, but thorougly proveable; and with all the varnishes and apologies, which this age of reason, refinement and revolutions, can put upon their conduct, the result of a fair investigation will produce juft fuch a conclufion.—To overdraw the character, or diftort the caufe in this ftage of it, would be a prejudice to the end which is aimed at. I have therefore prefented them as they muft appear, when record, evidence and fubftantial teftimony fhall be combined in the proof;—which will infallibly take place before the conclufion of this bufinefs. Let not thofe judge chimerical, this mode of introducing characters, who have obferved in courts of chancery every thing brought forward, which forms the characters of the parties, in direct relation to the caufe in queftion.—This is always admitted, and no more is contended.

THE fecond queftion to the plaintiffs, is—" What claim have you upon the juftice or equity of this court ?"—The anfwer muft be—" We have notes for our Georgia deeds, and we pray the power of the court to enforce the collection of them." The queftion to the defendants, is—" Did you fign and deliver thofe notes?—are they your act and deed?"—The anfwer is—" We did fign and deliver the notes; but they are not our act and deed?" At this inftant books, authorities, precedents all croud in favor of the plaintiffs: and a court poffeffed of full power to make a precedent of right, is to be ftormed out of all deliberation. But is every note, figned and delivered unconditionally, the act and deed of the figner?—fuppofe he is unable to read, and the note is read to him as for £.100, and it really is for £.1000, and can be fo proved, and that the obligee read it to him wrong,—is that his act and deed?—Again, fuppofe that he reads a note himfelf, and by fhuffling of the obligee, another is placed for him to fign, and he deliver the laft,—is that his act and deed?—Or if he figned and delivered it with a piftol at his breaft:—Are fuch notes the act and deed of thofe who deliver them?—Every one will agree no. Then there are cafes where a note may be figned and delivered unconditionally, and yet not be the act and deed of the figners.—Pray is there any difference between flight of hand and flight of head? Or shall he who reads a note wrong, and he who tells ten lies to obtain it, stand on a different footing?—Reason and common fense fay no. The books may be very nice about the mode in which the injured figner shall get rid of the payment; but they will never fupport a malefactor in recovering notes under these circumstances.

COURTS will not decide againft notes upon mere fuggeftion of fraud: It muft be made evident. In thefe cafes, various are the kinds and degrees of evidence; but when once it can be fhewn, that the plaintiff is one of the horde, or allied to thofe men who overrun thefe northern ftates with their Georgia fcrip or deeds, and that the confideration of the notes has wholly failed—the prefumption becomes violent, that thefe frauds have attended the fales; and that fmall portion of light and evidence, which almoft every individual purchafer can produce, will be fufficient to bring every cafe within the general principles and decifions, which muft obtain in all the Georgia caufes.

OUR courts and juries, if driven to peremptory law decifions, will decide that thefe notes are not the act and deed of the makers and deliverers of them. Sanguine Georgia fpeculators, who feel not the indignation and contempt which follows their enveloped frauds, may, under the pupilage of their lawyers, be taught to hope better things:—But let them remember, that great caufes draw forth the energy of man; and that on caufes of fuch magnitude, courts will do right. Hafte, negligence, confinement to nice conftructions, fometimes thwart the courfe of juftice, in fmall difputes; *but here no recovery can eventually be had, unless it shall appear eventually right, that men shall gain wealth by their own wrong.* I have here taken the

worft iffue which the caufes can poffibly be brought
to ; and if courts and juries will not, under the old
eftablifhment, determine againft the notes, yet when
the fellers knew they had no right in fee, and when it
appears by the event, that by reafon of their own fraud
they had no right at all,——courts and juries will determine againft the notes, whatever innovation it may
produce. Probably a decifion that thefe notes are not
the act and deed of the makers of them, upon the
ground that they were obtained by the groffeft deceit
of the obligee, would form a new precedent : but being bafed on right, it could never prejudice right in
any future decifions. The danger of new precedents
is, that the perverfenefs or ignorance of man may apply them where they ought not to be applied ; but this
danger, however great and often inculcated, has never
intimidated the independent judges in Weftminfter-
Hall from doing right, and making precedents where
juftice required them.

THESE remarks may apply to negotiable notes—to
Miffifippi fcript—to quit-claim deeds—and to all the
variety of cafes under thefe Georgia contracts.—For
if my premifes are right refpecting the original fraud,
and the total lofs of the lands, or the preemptive right
in the purchafers,—the conclufion will extend to every note and contract, iffuing from fuch a corrupt original.

THE cafe in refpect to the northern purchafers, is
precifely as if the firft grantees had forged the grant :
For, a grant voidable becaufe of fraud and corruption,
is no better nor worfe, than a forged one ;—and the
original actors in this fraud, and all their abettors,
confederates and acceffories, are every way as *bafely
guilty* as if they had forged the act.—The guilt as refpects the ftate of Georgia is the fame ; and the impo-
fition on the purchafers is certainly as great and per-
nicious. I call moft of thofe their confederates who

came from the midft of them, with their pamphlets
and mifreprefentations :—and even they, who were
themfelves deceived, and who deceived their neighbours, and are now prefling for great profits to themfelves, deferve an high rank in this brigade of impoftors. I fhould not affert thus pofitively on this fubject,
were I unable to bottom myfelf on the moft fubftantial proofs ;—and no individuals can be wounded by
fuch obloquies, but thofe whofe known conduct has
fully juftified them.

THESE remarks were not defigned to *add* any odi-
um to the fraudulent fellers of Georgia land ; but to
lead the minds of the purchafers, who have given their
notes, to reflect *on the whole Georgia bufinefs as a fyf-
tem of impofture and fwindling—on the refcinding act as
valid and conclufive—and on the power and difpofition of
our courts to do ample juftice on the fubject.* If the hints
fuggefted will lead to a new train of inveftigation, they
will anfwer the purpofe for which they were written.

NOTE.—The compafs which I have taken would not admit references to documents ; and the prefent ftage of the bufinefs rendered it improper to difcufs very minutely how the notes may
be avoided :—But thofe who hold deeds of Georgia land ought
to be thoroughly convinced, that all the lands now claimed under the ufurped act, are not worth one cent ;—and a pretence
that the refcinding act is void, is a miferable delufion.

Georgia Speculation Unveiled.

No. II.

FROM the premises in my first number, I open this with the following questions, and answers :—

1. DID the state of Georgia ever own the right in fee to the lands described in the granting act ?—Answer—No.

2. DID not the pretended claimants under the granting act publish and circulate a pamphlet, entitled,—" STATE OF FACTS,"—declaring the right of the state to have been a right in fee, and the sale of the state to have been fair and constitutional ?—Answer—They did.

3. WAS there any truth in these declarations ?—Answer—No.

4. WAS it not generally represented to the purchasers in these northern states, verbally as well as by said pamphlets, that the state of Georgia would not, and could not, rescind said grant ?—Answer—It was.

5. WAS there any truth in this representation ?—Answer—No.

6. Is not the grant rescinded in such manner, that the purchasers are wholly foreclosed of all possible benefit from their purchases, 'till the same sovereign will and power which rescinded the act, shall be united to restore it ?—Answer—Yes.

7. Is there any probability that they will ever voluntarily do this ?—Answer—Not the least.

8. CAN they be compelled to do it by any court or power in the United States ?—Answer—No.

9. Has not the state of Georgia by their refcinding act, put at great hazard the property, limbs and life of any man or body of men, who within the limits of faid ftate fhall in any way attempt to contravene faid act, or any claufe of it ?—Anfwer—Yes.

10. Have they not a fovereign right to make fuch laws as they judge proper for the well ordering of the ftate ?—Anfwer—They have.

11. If the declarations of the fellers and of their pamphlets had been true, would not the purchafes have been profitable to the purchafers ?—Anfwer—They probably would.

12. Falshood having been fubftituted in the place of truth, and the purchafers having relied on the declarations of the fellers, and thofe declarations having proved uniformly deceitful—fhall it be in the mouth of the fellers to fay to the purchafers—" You ought to have looked out that we did not cheat you ?"—Anfwer—No.

If any perfon is difpofed to give a different anfwer to any of thefe queftions, the queftion and anfwer fhall be made the fubject of a feparate difcuffion.

Several powerful delufions have been improved to crown the firft delufion.

1ft. That a grant is in its nature irreverfible.

2d. That provided the purchafers will ever have any claim on the fellers, they muft firft try the title which they have acquired ; and if that fails, then they may come upon the fellers.

3d. That thefe lands were purchafed as lottery tickets are, and if they had turned out fortunately, it would have been well with the purchafers : otherwife they muft bear the lofs.

4th. That all the book-principles relating to real eftate and to notes are in favor of the fellers, and that contefting the payment will be vain.

5th. That our courts will decide againft the refeinding act, and then the lands may be fold in Europe, for a dollar per acre.

6th. THAT the refcinding act was made in the tumult of the people, and that there is good chance of its being repealed, and the grant reftored.

7th. THAT if this refcinding act is good, the ftate of Connecticut may refcind the act granting the referve, and Maffachufetts their act granting the Cheneffee country.

By fuch chimeras, the advocates of the fales are addreffing themfelves to the hopes and fears, to the reafon and to the weaknefs of the purchafers ; and are thus endeavoring to wheedle them out of further payments. But be not deceived ;—for this irreverfible grant is actually reverfed, beyond the power of man ; and all the comparifons between the fovereign ftate of Georgia, granting their lands, and the province of New-Hampfhire, then fubject to Great-Britain, granting their lands, will be found vain. The diftinction muft be fuftained, that a dependant power has a power above them, to compel them to make good their grants and contracts ; and that *an independent power can make, or unmake grants at will; becaufe no power can decide on the morality, equity, or policy of their meafures.* If the granting act had been conftitutional, fair and honorable, and the refcinding act ever fo unfair and immoral,—yet the confequence to the purchafers would be equally fatal. The power which has deprived them of the lands, is beyond their control ; and all the advocates in favour of the fellers, never have and never can fuggeft one practicable mode of even beginning to attack the validity of the refcinding act. —That of deciding againft it in thefe northern ftates, has been already fhewn to be futile. Some have been difpofed to maintain, that if the firft act could be void at all, it muft have been fo in its own nature ; and therefore the refcinding act, notwithftanding the firft,

D

ſtands to be diſcuſſed on its own merits :—But this is only a re-production of the firſt deluſion ;—for the granting act does not ſtand at all : it is burnt, and that power alone, which could declare definitively on the validity of it, has put it beyond, the reach of diſ-cuſſion. The power itſelf is firſt to be diſcuſſed, and if you can once diſcuſs that out of exiſtence, you well know that the granting act will be good enough.— You have the parchments, 'tis true, large as dining-tables, certified by the ſecretary.—Vain ſhadows of a grant !—Dare you produce them in the ſtate of Geor-gia, to ſupport the title which you pretended to ſell us? Of little worth are they, if they cannot be produced on a trial, where if we obtain judgment, the execution will inveſt us with the title which you ſold us. A condition of wrong without redreſs, or of right with-out power, is very undeſirable to a landholder. Your own wrongs, your own frauds and violations of mo-rality, have led up this act, againſt which you ſo ve-hemently cry—ſhame, wickedneſs, immorality !—Go cry them in the ſtreets of Georgia, plead them in their courts, ring them in the ears of their legiſlators,—there alone will they anſwer our purpoſe. If this is all a fair tranſaction, as you declared to us by words and pamphlets, make it appear ſo to the world, and let us have the benefit of your exertions.—While it appears unfair and wicked, we ſhall withhold from you pay-ment—courts will ſuſtain us in withholding it :—and the certain event of the breaking of the bubble, will be your own bankruptcy, which is even now at the doors. I have not reſted entirely on the ground of power, thro' any idea that the granting act would be valid on its own merits. If any man judges that it was valid, and that the ſellers have conducted with a due portion of integrity, let him aſſert it ; and I am willing to take the burden of proving the act bad, and unfairly ob-tained,—and the conduct of a number of the ſellers to have been thoroughly abandoned.—In this number I include all those who were themselves deceived, and who in consequence deceived their neighbours, and who are demanding any profits in the trade. This fact of demanding *profits* in such a business, accompanied by a few acknowledged principles and deductions, will fix the character of such beyond a vindication.

I HAVE thus answered the two first delusions, and pray you to reflect, that the grant is really reversed and revoked, and that you can never try your title to any purpose—that you have lost all shadows of the land—and that if you have any defence to make, any money to save, any notes to avoid, or any redress to obtain,—now is your time ; and the time to avail yourselves will be short.

NEXT, as to the similitude between these sales, and those of lottery tickets, so often introduced, it may be just as respects a number of the Georgia bargains, so far as it can apply ; but if a man proposes to me to purchase of him a 100 tickets in the Savannah fire lottery, and shews me a scheme of the lottery, and assures me that it will be drawn in 60 days, and I buy them, and give him my note for the payment—and it afterwards appears that there was neither lottery, managers, nor any scheme published, or that there was a lottery without a prize, or one which could never be drawn,— am I to pay my note ?—Certainly not—especially not, if I can prove that this same man contrived with several others, to make out a scheme of a lottery, which could not in its nature answer any other purposes than those of imposture. But this comparison with lottery tickets is not just : for in lottery tickets, every man buys with known hazard of loss or gain. In these bargains every man bought with the greatest certainty of gain, provided the pamphlets and declarations which he bought with his deeds, proved true.—He could not calculate upon lofs, except from thofe circumftances of treachery and fraud on the part of the fellers, which would wholly vacate the contract.

BUT 4th. Thofe who have given notes, are to be frightened by the books!!—Unfortunately for the fellers, the books give no comfort, no fupport. Courts have been trammelled by books at the opening of this bufinefs.—Judge Chafe was trammelled with books in the opening of the famous Connecticut ftate caufe; but after four days digeftion, his mind was relieved, and he declared that the books did not apply, and that there was *no fuch thing as fuftaining an analogy between protections granted by a fovereign independent ftate, and thofe granted by the dependant courts of Weftminfter-Hall.* By citing books and authorities, and covering the green cloth with folios, the advocates may perfuade their Georgia clients, that much good may come out of evil; but on thorough canvaffing, it will be found, that (ftrange to tell) the books can afford no light on a fubject of which the compilers had no conception.

5th. LET purchafers be guarded againft being amufed by the profpect of *our* courts deciding againft the refcinding act.—If all the courts in the United States fhould decide againft it, and all the marfhalls and deputy-marfhalls, fheriffs and deputy-fheriffs, fhould be employed to carry their judgments into effect,—the whole would ftill be a miferable farce and delufion; —for they would not in the leaft prejudice the refcinding act, nor benefit our title, and the ftate of Georgia would care nothing about them.

6th. As to the refcinding act being made in the tumult of the people, and that there is good chance of its being repealed—there is not one word of truth, nor fymptom of probability about it:—and this pretence is a mere continuation of the falfe and fwindling meafures, which have been practifed on you.

AND 7th. As to the hypothetical reafoning, that if

Georgia could refcind this act, then Connecticut and Maffachufetts can refcind theirs—it ought to be otherwife ftated, viz.—That Georgia has refcinded her granting act, and if Connecticut and Maffachufetts fhould refcind theirs, they would do as Georgia has done;—and what would the claimants do in any fuch cafe, where the Indian title is not extinguifhed? In a fituation wholly remedilefs, as to title or preemption, are you who have thought yourfelves purchafers of Georgia lands; and your fituation is brought on you by your confidence in thofe, who fold to you;—and this fituation is aggravated by the perfecutions and law perplexities, with which thefe deceivers are hunting you. Your time is devoted, and your property fubjected to the apparent rapacity of the Georgia fellers; but they in reality, are now only the puppets of the farce—there is not one chance in a thoufand of their eventually gaining any thing; but ftill the farce muft be carried on, for the emolument of the craftsmen. Of great importance is it in this fituation, that you poffefs yourfelves of facts—that you give way to no delufions —and that you compofe yourfelves under thefe complicated abufes. If you get rid of your notes, yet the land deeded to you is not worth a thoufandth part of what you have paid—be that fum ever fo fmall.

As many of the ideas, which have been introduced on this fubject, tending to fhew that the common law principles and practice cannot be applied to thefe cafes, may appear inadmiffible,—I beg leave to enforce them by reference to the reafonings and practice adopted in the South fea fcheme, in the year 1721.*

" WHEN the bubble burft, and the ftock the fub-
" fcribers had purchafed at 1000 per cent. fell to 150,
" and of courfe the lofs of every fuch fubfcriber was
" £.850 out of every £.1000 fubfcribed—I fay, when

* See Tindal's continuation of Rapin, under the words, South Sea Trade and Company.

" this happened, legal fuits (of which very many were
" commenced) for thefe debts, due to the company,
" would have reduced moft of the monied men in the
" kingdom, to a ftate of remedilefs bankruptcy, and
" the company muft have loft moft of their money
" in the bargain. The public creditors had loft moft
" of their public fecurities, which they had fubfcribed
" into that fund,—and infinite other mifchiefs of a like
" nature muft have accrued of a kind moft ruinous
" and wrong, and of an amount fo great as to affect
" national Intereft, honor and credit, and of fuch an
" extreme and extraordinary nature, that no ordinary
" rules of law could be applied in any fuch manner as
" to afford the leaft remedy ; but would rather in-
" creafe the evil, and give the wrong a kind of fanc-
" tion of the law.

" In this extreme cafe, the parliament found them-
" felves under an abfolute neceffity of affuming the
" power of fovereign equity, and as fupreme chancel-
" lors of the kingdom to fuperfede the ordinary rules
" of the law, control its force, foften its rigor, and a-
" dopt fuch equitable principles as would afford fome
" remedy of an evil, an injury, a wrong of fuch mag-
" nitude as brought the juftice, credit and fafety of
" the nation into danger. On this principle, they fuf-
" pended law-fuits, annulled fpecial bails, difcharged
" numberlefs debtors who owed for ftock, on paying
" 10 per cent. of their debts, compelled compenfa-
" tions in favor of the fufferers, forced dividends and
" appropriations of the ftock of the company, and e-
" ven punifhed many for mifmanagement, who feem-
" ed to have conformed themfelves to the letter of the
" law," &c. &c. &c.

Very ftrong remonftrances were made againft the
interference of the legiflature, and that the matter
fhould be left to the courfe of law, i. e. to be decided
according to the common rule of affignments of all

negotiable notes, bonds, &c.—but on a clofe infpection of the matter, it was foon clearly feen, that the variation of the exchange of thefe ftocks (or their depreciation, as we call it) was fo enormous and extreme, that any application of the ordinary rules of law and practice, to them, would produce the moft ruinous injuftice and wrongs,—and of courfe, every idea of that mode of fettlement and adjuftment was inftantly given up. Their great principle was, that juftice and right was the grand end of law, and paramount to any particular rules, or eftablifhed practice,—and of courfe, ought to control them in all cafes of fo extreme and extraordinary a kind, as could not fall within the reafon on which thefe rules were founded ; but fo circumftanced as that an application of thefe common rules, would unavoidably produce fuch injury and wrong, as was totally deftructive of all that right, which was the effential principle and end of all laws.

As a further explanation of the interference of parliament, it was faid that collections according to the common rule of affignments, " would bring remedilefs ruin on thoufands of individuals, and at the fame time heap immenfe fortunes on others, who had never deferved them."

VERY fimilar to this, in operation and management, was the Miffiffippi bubble, in France, two years before. In both thefe important and memorable precedents, of two of the moft enlightened nations in the world, were recognized fpecifically the following principles—"That the ordinary rules of law would do infinite mifchief and injuftice, were not the rigor of them to be foftened and corrected by chancery—that the powers of chancery ought always to control the common law, whenever in any cafe the application of the ordinary rules of law, will manifeftly deftroy right and juftice, or work a wrong—that law is certainly perverted, and needs correction, whenever it deftroys right or does wrong." That the fupreme power of every ftate, is the fupreme chancery of it, and muft have fovereign authority to repeal, to limit or control every rule of law, and may and ought to do it, whenever that rule operates by way of deftruction or defalcation of right, or producing of wrong,—and that juftice and fecurity of right can never be perfect or even tolerable in any ftate, without the exiftence of this power and the pru‑ dent exercife of it.*

These are vital iffues from the fource of law, calcu‑ lated to do good, wherever they flow :—thefe are prin‑ ciples, which put to flight all tecknical diftinctions, and furnifh us with a truth highly important in thefe cauf‑ es, viz.—that there are extraordinary cafes, where com‑ mon law principles cannot and ought not to be appli‑ ed, by reafon of the manifeft injuftice, which would refult from an application of them.

These Georgia caufes furnifh the ftrongeft inftance fince 1721, for the application of thefe principles.— They do not precifely refemble either of the other bub‑ bles : for in the South fea fcheme, the amazing rife of the ftock, originated in their contract with parliament, for taking in the national debt. Their ftate of prof‑ perity was overrated, and the funds rofe by mere en‑ thufiafm, from 130 to 330 per cent.—and from the month of April to Auguft, they rofe from the laft fum to 1000 per cent ; but it was a reality they were deal‑ ing in :—and even after the bubble broke and parlia‑ ment interfered, the ftock was really worth 150 per cent. It will be well feen, that the Georgia bubble does not precifely refemble that of the South fea :— for here was no reality at bottom, and here was great fraud in the means, as I conftantly hold myfelf ref‑ ponfible to fhew, whenever it fhall be doubted.—But in one very important refpect, there is a refemblance.

* For thefe remarks on the South Sea bubble, fee Peletiah Web‑ fter's Political Effays, page 334.

The legiſlature of the ſtate of Georgia, like the ſovereign legiſlatures of England and France, ſeeing the
wrong and oppreſſion, which would be cauſed by the
collection of the notes, and combining this with the
other inducements before ſtated—have, as they had a
ſovereign right to do, deſtroyed the whole conſideration of the notes, and have thus let them and the holders of them to the ground. The ſovereign legiſlature of the union, might have ſuſpended the power of
their own courts, from any cognizance of the cauſes :
ſo the legiſlatures of the ſeveral ſtates might have ſuſpended the power of their courts ; but this would have
been only a partial remedy of the evil. The ſtate of
Georgia, whoſe acts and laws are to be reſpected thro'-
out the union, has in a moſt pointed and peremptory
manner declared, that there is no conſideration for
theſe notes,—and has ſhewn the neceſſity and propriety of this declaration more concluſively, than they
were ſhewn by either of thoſe parliaments. Their
exerciſe of ſovereignty is not novel, and the reaſons
on which it is founded are as old as the world.—
*This public act of the ſtate of Georgia, is the beſt and moſt
concluſive teſtimony of a want of conſideration, which can
be improved in a court of chancery : and thoſe courts could
never have granted relief againſt notes for want of conſideration, on more ample grounds.*

In a very important reſpect alſo, the Georgia plaintiffs ſtand in the ſame rank with thoſe, who in the
South ſea buſineſs were proſecuting for $\frac{850}{1000}$ of what
coſt them nothing, and was good for nothing :—the
remaining $\frac{150}{1000}$ and the price actually paid for the
lands by the Georgia companies, placing them both on
an equal footing,—both having a law of a ſovereign
ſtate, barring them from an oppreſſive recovery—and
both equally deſerving to feel the inconvenience reſult-
ing to oppreſſors from the operation of principles of
equity.—Neither can be in the rank of thoſe, who

F

hold notes for money lent, or labour done ; but both are in the rank of thofe, who are hunting for money, on principles deftructive to the defign of courts, and the exiftence of fociety. It is fortunate for the public, that there fhould be fuch a concurrence of public acts of fovereign legiflatures, on fubjects fo fimilar—and that the parties prefling for payment at the bar of our courts, fhould meet an obftacle fo equally and juftly fatal to their unfounded claims : for the decifions in thefe cafes againft the notes, will give to our courts occafion to affert principles deftructive to the fraudulent arts, which have expofed many of our citizens to fevere lofs of property.

HAPPILY our courts are not deftitute of chancery powers, fufficient to carry the equitable objects of the refcinding act into full effect : and when the doctrines of chancery are introduced—when the original principles of right are contemplated—when this bubble is compared with other bubbles—when the parties and the caufes are known, and the refcinding act is duly plead,—if courts can hefitate about pronouncing a-gainft the notes, it will be only that one fiat of the national legiflature, may put a perpetual end to the convulfions and diftrefs caufed by the Georgia, Virginia, Sufquehannah, Canada, and all other bafelefs fpeculations.

IT will be well feen, that I have not left thefe notes to depend on the contingence of fuch a national meafure. The defence of thofe, who are fued on their notes, ftands moft fubftantially on the chancery powers vefted in our courts :—and the means of calling thofe powers into effectual exercife, have been juft fhewn to be abundant.

BUT merely to get rid of the payment of the notes is not the fole object.—Large fums of money have been paid, which in equity and good confcience ought to be refunded.—In addition to thefe, great damages have been fuftained, by reafon of the falfhood and fwindling practifed in thefe fales. The lands or deeds in the hands of the purchafers, are not worth a farthing,—and would be worth the meereft trifle, if the refcinding act fhould now be burnt, and the granting act reftored :—for the granting act reftored would not inveft you with the fee of the lands, fubject to the right of hunting and fifhing, &c.—which fee you thought yourfelves to have bought : and the violent parties, which have been created in the confufion of this bufinefs, would probably prevent your ever obtaining a right to extinguifh the Indian title.—Indeed the commotions about the Georgia lands, have led up a ferious claim of congrefs,—which otherwife would have been as dormant as their claim to the Cheneffee country.—This claim, however originated, will not be eafily relinquifhed.

But if all obftacles were removed, your right to hold a treaty, is merely a right to buy the land at the full value of it,—and this you are to do under the eye of fworn commiffioners and interpreters. This treaty is to be opened with great expenfe : and your agents are to meet not a few ignorant ftraggling Indians, but the powerful, opulent and enlightened nations of the Creeks, Chactaws and Chickafaws—headed by chiefs of great fame, information and influence.—The object of this treaty is, to buy from them the place of their birth, their conquefts and their refidence :—and you come to them under the fafcinating character of men, reprefenting a horde of impoftors, who cheated the reprefentatives of the ftate of Georgia, out of their ufurped and impofing right of alone bidding on thefe lands : and you apply to them, after blood has been repeatedly and unfuccefsfully fhed, to force them to retreat.—You apply to them for their lands—not as a place of refuge from perfecution—not as a foil, where you wifh to labour, and to introduce agriculture, and the arts of civilized life—not as a place, where you wish to embrace and treat them as a band of brothers ;—but as a frontier, where you may erect forts, establish garrisons, stretch the strong arm of the union, and fill, with their ancient and implacable oppressors and enemies.—With a council such as these nations will present to you,—rum, whisky and rusty nails, will not be considered as conclusive arguments :—truth, sincerity and a sufficiency of property to enable them to remove where they may do better, will alone go down. Will you tell them, that you have already paid large sums of money, to prevent others from bidding on their lands—and that therefore you cannot give the full value of them ?—Will you desire the commissioners to inform them, that you expect to make immense fortunes out of their lands, and that there is no way of your doing it, but by purchasing them for far less than they are worth ?—Shall your interpreters expound to them the whole history of this business ?—Or will you smoke with them the calumet of peace, exchange your baubles for theirs, and call them friends and brothers ? Will you tell them, that you came from a land flowing with milk and honey, abounding in corn and green pastures, and overflowing in all the conveniences and luxuries of life—from a land, where every industrious man may gain wealth—and that for their sakes you are come up thither ? They know better than all this,—they have lately told us, at lake Erie, that they know the arts of the white men :—and the Georgia commissioners, but last year, with as much parade as could attend a treaty, and as plausible talks as you can hold with them, got for answer, that they would not sell.—And suppose you get the same answer, after all your expenses, what is your preemption worth ?—Or suppose they should offer the lands to you, at such price as you have repeatedly declared them worth, if free from incumbrance, what would your preemption be

worth ?   As refpects the Indians, the lands are theirs
in fee, with all the ufes belonging to them ;—and they
care not for preemptive rights—they can difencumber
them at pleafure—and they feel and know themfelves
entitled to as much in value, as the lands are worth to
any purchafer,—and there is no propriety in their giving you 9-10ths of the whole land for felling the re-
mainder :—and yet a lefs commiffion for doing this
bufinefs, is hardly contemplated.   Perhaps fraud or
force may deprive thefe nations of their lands, within
a few years ; but I have no idea, that within a centu-
ry they will voluntarily fell them :—for they are not
a miferable handful, as the Georgia fellers reprefented,
conftantly decreafing in numbers, and rather inclining
to retreat than to maintain their ground ; but juft the
contrary.

SHALL it be faid, that the purchafers knew or ought
to have known all thefe things ?—The beft anfwer will
be, that they did not know them, and had not the
means of knowing them, and the whole reprefentation
was as I have before ftated—that there was only an
ufufruct between the purchafers and a complete poffeffion of the lands,—which ufufruct might be eafily
extinguifhed, as there were immenfe tracts farther to
the weftward and northward, where the Indians would
find better hunting and fifhing than on thefe lands.—
The commotions refpecting the fales have been fuch,
that a reftoration of the granting act, if fuch an event
could be conceived, would be very far from reftoring
to the prefent claimants, what they fuppofed they had
purchafed :—fo far from it, that the incumbrances then
exifting upon the claim, would in all probability be in-
furmountable.   I have not even taken into my calcu-
lation, the influence which the ftate of Georgia, or a-
ny party among them, might ufe againft you in cafe
of a treaty,—nor the probable exiftence of a great interference of titles, by fraudulent and multiplied deeds,

resting merely on detached paper or parchment, without any record to support them or discover their fal-
lacy ;—but we have a fair right to believe, that men
who will take unprincipled means to get rich, will not
be less abandoned in the means of extrication, when
the gulph of bankruptcy is before them.

In VIEW of the premises, I fully believe, that a res-
toration of the granting act, would not only wrong
the people of Georgia,—but would prove a serious e-
vil to the present claimants, and a dreadful misfortune
to all who might be after purchasers.—It would open
a new scene of delusive hopes to the world, and fur-
nish new daggers to aim at the vitals of morality, fair
dealing and confidence between man and man. Long
enough have friends stabbed friends, neighbours be-
trayed neighbours—and the wealth of centuries been
wasted by the delusions of a moment.—Truth, hones-
ty and commercial credit have suffered wounds deep
enough : and all the friends of society feel grateful to
the legislature, which arrested in its progress the des-
tructive pestilence. Formerly the enemies of man fre-
quented the public roads—put pistols to the breasts of
unsuspecting travellers, and robbed them of the valu-
ables they had about them ; but the sufferers could re-
turn to their houses and lands, and by industry repair
the loss.—We live to see robbery in a more refined
stile. Men who never added an iota to the wealth or
morals of the world, and whose single moment was
never devoted to making one being wiser or happier
throughout the universe—riding in their chariots—
plotting the ruin of born and unborn millions—aiming with feathers to cut throats, and on parchments
to seal destruction,—these are the robbers of modern
days.—They bring desolation among our farmers—
they spread distress in towns—they scorn the paltry
plunder of pocket-books, and watches—they aim at
houses and lands—strike at the foundation of many

generations,—and would deftroy families, root and branch. Long enough have fraud, falfhood and fwindling ftalked our ftreets :—often enough have our farmers left their fields and wrecked the induftry of painful and honeft years upon the mountains of Virginia : —often enough have our jails and dockets witneffed the ruined hopes of the dupes of Newtown and Stockbridge fpeculations.—Thefe laft are not imputable to the Georgia fellers,—unlefs by their fuperior addrefs, and the wider ruin they have caufed, they may claim the honor of ingurgitating thefe leffer robberies.

I am not diftorting this fubject ; but am drawing likeneffes of which the originals exift. The indignation of an incenfed public, is faft gathering over you who have fat for this picture.—The advocates of your impoftures, begin to difcover, that they have been led to abet meafures which they abhor. The means of paying fees are nearly exhaufted—the funds to whch you look for help, will prove as deceitful as the eyes of thofe, whom you have injured, will be dreadful to you, after your ruin fhall be complete. Your characters, your hopes of wealth, your all, are tumbling into the pit, which you have digged for others :—and if the day of your total poverty, contempt and defpair, can be haftened by what is here written, I fhall have paid to you, who deferve this character, the only debt, which in equity and good confcience I owe you.

New-Haven, Oct. 14, 1797.   A. B.

[*The documents and authorities on which thefe pages are founded, will in due time be prefented to the public.*]